Journey Through History

The Middle Ages

Translation: Jean Grasso Fitzpatrick

English translation © Copyright 1988 by Barron's Educational Series, Inc.

© Parramón Ediciones, S.A.
First Edition, February 1988
The title of the Spanish edition is *La edad media*

All inquiries should be addressed to:
Barron's Educational Series, Inc.
250 Wireless Boulevard
Hauppauge, New York 11788

Library of Congress Catalog Card No. 88-10384
International Standard Book No. 0-8120-3386-8
Library of Congress Cataloging-in-Publication Data

Vergés, Gloria.
  [Edad Media. English]
  The Middle Ages / [illustrated by] María Rius; [written by]
Gloria & Oriol Vergés; [translation, Jean Grasso Fitzpatrick].—1st ed.
    p. cm.—(Journey through history)
  Translation of: Edad Media.
  Summary: An illustrated history of the Middle Ages, with a
fictional story involving children to depict the time in history.
  ISBN 0-8120-3386-8
  1. Middle Ages–History—Juvenile literature. [1. Middle Ages—
History.] I. Rius, María, ill. II. Vergés, Oriol. III. Title. IV. Series:
Vergés, Gloria. Viaje a través de la historia. English.
D117.V4713 1988
940.1—dc19   88-10384
                                                               CIP
                                                               AC

Printed in Spain by Sirven Grafic
Legal Deposit: B-39.932-88

Journey Through History

The Middle Ages

María Rius
Glòria & Oriol Vergés

BARRON'S

New York · Toronto · Sydney

In three days we will be through with the harvest," said Father. "Luckily, this year the crop has been good. Now we must thresh the grain and store it in the silo, before the rain and cold come."

"And this year there will be no plague, God willing!" answered Mother. "With the silo full, we won't go hungry this winter. Do you know what we ought to do? Trade a couple of bags of grain with our neighbors in exchange for some of their bacon."

The children were delighted with this proposal. Life for peasants in the Middle Ages was very hard, and eating even a little bit of meat was a special treat.

The few peasants who owned their own land traded what they produced for what they needed. This kind of swapping, called *barter*, was done either with neighbors or at the town market. Things were rarely bought for money because copper, silver, and gold coins were very scarce. Paper money did not exist.

Peasants who didn't own land were called *serfs*. They had to live in cottages near the fields they worked, and they could not move from there.

"What a sad life our parents lead!" said the boy.

"And us, too," replied the girl, "because when we grow up, we'll be serfs like them!"

"Well, when I'm a little older, I'm going to run away!" said the boy. "I'll find a place where no one knows me...and I'll be free!"

"Our neighbors son thought he could do that, but the baron's hunting dogs followed his trail. When the knights caught up with him, they put him in a dungeon and beat him....Who knows when he'll go free!"

In the monasteries, the monks led a quieter life than that of the peasants. The abbott presided over the community, and the prior organized the monks' day, which was divided between prayers and work.

"For me, the hardest thing is to get up when it's still dark and cold, after having slept on a bed of straw," said Brother John.

"Remember that everything we suffer is for the love of God. He will reward us," replied Brother Thomas.

"Have you seen the painting behind the main alter of the chapel? I've been helping Father Bernard prepare the colors for three days!"

"Do you know how to paint?"

"Of course! When the paintings are finished and the peasants come to church and see them, they will learn about the lives of Jesus and Mary. Every day I work until the bell rings to call us to evening prayer."

Since they were the only people who knew how to read and write, the monks spent many hours sitting at their desks in the library, or *scriptorium*. There they copied religious books and colored the initial letter of each chapter. Sometimes they made illustrations for the texts.

"Have you finished your work in the chapel?" asked Brother Thomas.

"Yes, but since I did such a good job mixing colors, the prior has given me some illustrations to do," answered Brother John.

"Aren't you lucky!" replied Brother Thomas. "Today I have to accompany the priest who visits the peasants that take care of our monastery's lands. We have to make sure they give us our fair share of the harvest.... If that is God's will, of course!"

The nobles were always declaring war on each other, and the peasants suffered because of it.

"How lucky we are! The enemy soldiers haven't burned down our house," exclaimed one woman. "But, what difference would it really make? It's not much better than a pig sty!"

"What a shame!" answered another. "And all because the count is angry with our baron!"

When the landlords fought, the peasants hid in the castle courtyard, where they felt safe within the fortified walls.

The noble lord chose the strongest men from among his under-lords, called *vassals*, and made them knights in his army.

When a nobleman was not off to war, he kept in training by hunting. He and his men rode on horseback and practiced using arrows and spears.

"What a good horseman the count's son is!" said one child. "In a few years he'll ride with his father when he goes off to wars."

"But his brother, the count's younger son, is learning to read and write in the monastery. You know, if he becomes a monk, he might end up being an abbott—or even a bishop!"

"If he does, he would have as much power and be just as important as his father!"

Later on, people decided to live in cities. Serfs went there in order to escape from the lords of the castles. If they succeeded, they tried to get under the protection of the lord mayor, an important noble, or a bishop. These rulers usually offered better treatment than did the lords of the castles.

"Inside these thick walls and strong doors," said the peasant on his way to the market, "I feel a lot safer. It's not as dangerous to live in the city as it is in the country."

"Halt! Where are you going?" asked the soldier.

"Don't you recognize us?" the peasant asked. "We come to sell our vegetables every week. Don't worry. At the end of the month we will pay our taxes in real silver!"

The market, situated in the center of the town, was a lively place. The merchants called out their wares, and the customers haggled over prices.

"Buy, buy! Silks from China that just arrived yesterday!"

"Boxes and chests! Made of good wood, in all different sizes!"

"Fine spices! Cinnamon, saffron! They will make your food taste like the delicacies of the royal palace!"

"If I were rich, do you know what I would do?" asked a boy. "I would buy one thing from each merchant! But there's no point in dreaming. I'm the son of an ordinary carpenter, and I'm sure to grow up to be a carpenter myself."

"Look at these fine daggers! The merchant is Spanish and he told me that they were made out of the best steel in Europe."

"Take these back, master shoemaker," the woman said. "They're the shoes that you made for me two days ago. They've already got a hole in them."

"How strange!" the shoemaker exclaimed. "This is the most expensive material from France!"

"This shoemaker is the best in the city," explained the boy. "He works for all of the nobles. The shoes he and his assistant make are very handsome, and they usually last a long time."

In those days, all of the shoemakers worked in shops clustered on the same street. They all belonged to the same club called a *guild*. Craftsmen in the other trades had their own street and their own guild. That's why, in the old neighborhoods of some European cities, you still see streets with the names of those guilds from the Middle Ages: Shoemakers Lane, Jewelers Alley, Tanners Place....

"Have you seen what a nice suit my uncle is wearing?" asked the boy, pointing. "He bought it in Venice the last time he was there. When I grow up I'm going to sail from one city to another, too."

"What are they carrying on that ship?" asked his friend.

"That depends," he answered. "If they're going to northern Europe, it will be oil, wheat, and wine. There they buy fine woolens and linen, embroidered with gold and silver. If they're going to the Orient, they buy silks, ivory, and spices."

"I'm going to be a merchant, too! But, because I get seasick, I'll take the land routes, with a mule caravan."

During the Middle Ages, trade by land and sea was very important in Europe. The merchants followed standard routes and sold their goods in the markets of the great cities and at country fairs.

In the great hall of the castles, poets, called *troubadours*, recited and sang poems in praise of the ladies of the court. Jugglers, dancers, and musicians also performed for the nobles.

"Look, the knights are on their horses. They're getting ready for a jousting contest, after the poetry competition," said the boy. "It's going to be really exciting!"

"The knight with the red flag is going to win," the girl assured him. "Last year he did very well."

Meanwhile, the troubadour, who had just arrived from France, continued to sing.

"Shh, don't make a sound!" the girl warned. "Today the court is meeting. I think the nobles are going to complain to the king because his soldiers have been going on their lands."

"The soldiers can't do that, can they?" asked her young brother. "No, it's against the king's law," she answered. "And look—the bishops and merchants from the city are also here, asking that only ships flying our flag be allowed to drop anchor in the port."

"That makes sense! Otherwise they would lose business to the foreign merchants!"

"Look how happy the master stone cutter is! I've never seen him smile that way!" said the boy.

"My father says the king, the bishop, and the guilds have agreed to pay him more money to work on the cathedral," said the girl.

"And my big brother, who is an architect, told me that the bell tower will be much taller than the one in the next city."

"We'll certainly be able to boast about our cathedral!" the boy exclaimed. "And that's not all! They're putting in stained-glass windows that will allow the sun to pass through and make all sorts of designs on the floor."

Gothic cathedrals, which are still the pride of many European cities, were built through the efforts of all the inhabitants. The amazing height and great beauty of the interiors encouraged everyone to gather together and pray.

As far as art, daily life, economics, and politics are concerned, the Middle Ages can be divided into two very different periods. The early Middle Ages extended from the fall of the Roman Empire until the twelfth century. The later Middle Ages lasted until the fifteenth century, when the Renaissance began.

Peasant Life

Rural life was poor, and the peasants survived by bartering their produce in the village markets for other foods or for clothing, since money was scarce. Some of the peasants owned the lands they cultivated and could leave them to their children, but the majority were serfs of the feudal lords.

The Monasteries

The monks prayed and led a very strict life most of the day. The Benedictines taught farming techniques—which had been almost forgotten at that time—to the peasants, who then cultivated the monastery lands. Through the construction of monasteries, the monks also inspired the expansion of Romanesque art—which was midway between the earlier Roman and the later Gothic styles.

The Preservation of Culture

The cultural richness of classical antiquity had almost been forgotten, and the important task of recovering it was being carried out in the monasteries. The monks were virtually the only ones who knew how to read and write. In the *scriptoria* of the monasteries they copied sacred texts or classical works on parchment and illustrated them with miniature drawings.

Feudalism

The feudal lord was given a territory by the king and was supposed to defend it. For this reason his main occupation was war. In times of peace, he spent his days hunting and participating in tournaments. In all the castles there were small armies of knights on horseback and foot-soldiers. The soldiers wore coats of armor and carried swords and lances.

Life in the Cities

One of the main characteristics of the later Middle Ages was the rise in population in the cities. The inhabitants of towns dedicated themselves mainly to trade and crafts. They were freer than the serfs of the feudal lords.

The Guilds

The cities saw a growth of many different crafts. The artisans worked in small shops under the direction of a master craftsman. The guilds were associations of craftspeople with the same specialty (embroiderers, silversmiths, printers, etc.), who defended their members from abuses of power by the nobles and made sure they had plenty of work.

Commerce in the Later Middle Ages

The growth of commerce made it possible for many city dwellers to "get rich quick." Furthermore, the advances in navigation technique permitted them to make long voyages in search of new markets, which in turn gave them opportunities to make vast sums of money. These were deposited in the early banks.

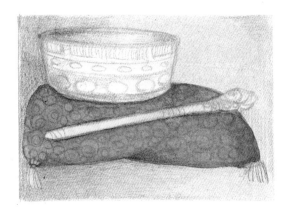

The Medieval Courts

The medieval courts brought a refinement of customs. Jugglers performed, and the troubadours recited and sang their poetry. The poetry competitions alternated with jousting tournaments in which the knights demonstrated their skill in handling their weapons.